UNDERSTANDING
PAKISTANI
— CULTURE —

UNDERSTANDING
PAKISTANI
— CULTURE —

NAEEM HARRY

authorHOUSE®

AuthorHouse™
1663 Liberty Drive
Bloomington, IN 47403
www.authorhouse.com
Phone: 1-800-839-8640

Published by AuthorHouse   11/02/2012

ISBN: 978-1-4772-8687-6 (sc)
ISBN: 978-1-4772-8686-9 (e)

Library of Congress Control Number: 2012920715

I would like to dedicate this book to my wife, Mariam Nawab.

CONTENTS

INTRODUCTION

There are millions of Pakistanis living throughout the world, and from time to time they will need medical, spiritual, and psychological care. This can only be successfully given if their culture is understood.

My thought is that I begin my book, Understanding Pakistani Culture, with an explanation that I am from Pakistan and I now live in the United States. I am a spiritual counselor who visits patients in hospitals to help them, and sometimes I encounter patients born in Pakistan. Because their customs are often so different from US customs, those wishing to help do not understand their needs. My thought has been to write a book about Pakistani customs to bring forward the understanding.

Do you know that Pakistanis prefer never to eat alone? There are always one or two people present. One of my friends shared this story with me when she was hospitalized in Rochester, New York. An elderly Pakistani woman who spoke no English was sharing my friend's semi-private room and the old woman refused to eat. Nurses and hospital staff urged her but she would not. It became a worry. Fortunately, it was pointed out to the hospital staff that someone needed to sit with the woman while she ate her meals. This was an important Pakistani custom. And so, someone sat with her at mealtime and the old woman began to eat. The problem was solved.

Again, there are millions of Pakistanis living throughout the world and care for some will be needed. This can only be successfully given if the culture is understood.

CHAPTER 1

FAMILIES

Elders are Leaders

Elders are respected by all family members who are younger than they are and they are like a father or uncle to everyone. An elder is under no obligation to respect younger family members, but he should love every member. Even if he scolds or insults, this must be tolerated because it is understood that he is teaching.

They are never called by name. Instead, they are called an uncle or aunt. If someone calls them by name, this is considered disrespectful. Eye contact with an elder is forbidden because he holds power and must not be challenged. Eye contact would be the first step toward disobedience and disrespect.

Pakistanis normally do not make their own decisions, and instead, decisions are made by male elders. There are no independent decisions. Every decision has an influence on a family, and so every decision comes from the family, not from an individual.

Male Earnings

Generally it is the male's earnings that support the family. When a family consists of more than seven members, one person's earnings cannot support the whole family. Normally, the income is not more than thirty dollars a month and a large family will create a problem. Everyone is under an obligation to support the family in some manner. This is a sacred obligation. People sacrifice to keep this obligation. Once one is born into a family, there is no separation until one breathes his last breath. If a daughter cannot support the family financially, she will support it morally.

Culturally, the concept of self care does not exist because all family members live for each other, and each must look after the other. If one is sick, he has to be looked after by the other family members. Every moment of his life is to be lived for others, not for himself. No one can claim that it is his time to die. Every life and energy is for each other.

Male and Recognition

A Pakistani male is recognized as a male if he is able to feed his family. His wife may be employed and earning money, but still, her husband will only be recognized as a male if he is able to bring income home.

Husband and Wife Relationship

Culturally, the wife is subordinate to the husband and she has to obey his orders. To be a good wife, she must understand very well the art of obedience. If she does not obey, there are consequences. The husband is under no obligation to his wife, and because he is considered above his wife, he does not have to listen to her.

Men at Home

Husband and wife responsibilities are divided in Pakistani society. It is not the husband's responsibility to help his wife at home, and the majority of husbands will sit and watch their wives cleaning and cooking. Women train males not to work at home because it is insulting.

Fathers

Traditionally, families in Pakistan follow a strict way of living. Today, however, the the electronic media show cultures that are free and modern and different from the traditional culture of Pakistan. This difference begins to cause problems for a Pakistani male who will become a father. Now, a potential father may go through the following stages:

Before marriage, he dreams of having a beautiful bride who will care for him, his future children, and his household as a joint family. He dreams he will have children, preferably two boys and two girls, and he plans to educate them without any discrimination.

After marriage, he begins his life with his wife and children. He loves equally his male and female children and he tries to provide equal opportunities to them.

When his children reach the age of sixteen, he knows his daughters will begin to act like adults and they will want to be adults. Now he begins discrimination. His daughters will be forbidden to go out of the house, and they will be forbidden to be familiar and have fun with males outside the family. He, as the father, is the head of the house, and he must make decisions for his daughters regarding studies, marriage, and jobs. Now, his daughters will silently begin to agitate against the realization they have no hope. They understand their life is one of lifelong dependence.

Life of a Widower

The life of a widower becomes very complex. He has to do all the duties his wife has been doing. He has to be a father and a mother. He has to provide both maternal and paternal love. He learns to cook and to clean and he will be teased by his friends when they see him doing this for his children. Most widowers remarry but some do not. Because he is a male, the life of an unmarried one is not as miserable as that of a widow.

Most Family Women are Homebound

Most women living in Pakistani cities stay home. They work at home and care for their children, and they also care for the elders at home. They cook, clean and take care of the needs of visitors. In the morning they will sweep with brooms and also they will sweep many times throughout the day. They will not sweep the house after sunset because this is considered unfortunate for the prosperity of the house. Men do not sweep the house. They sweep the streets if they work for the municipality, but it would be disrespectful for males to sweep the house.

Mothers are not Challenged

Generally, people do not challenge and go against the will of mothers. Her position in the hierarchy of the family is highly respectable, and she is such an important figure in the family, she cannot be challenged

Women and Dependency

Pakistani women are trained to be dependent on males. Today there is an independence movement by women, but it is considered an insult in a male- dominated society. Those who want to be independent will face many challenges and hardships. Women who are dependent are considered respectful. It is understood that the dependency of a female puts a burden on the male, but the male accepts this.

Woman Earnings

Culturally and psychologically, a Pakistani woman believes that there is no blessing in her income if she works. There is only blessing in the income of a male because males dominate society. If a male does not bring money into the house, there is no blessing in the house.

Girls Work Hard

Girls in Pakistan are very hardworking. Because they have no opportunity for recreation, they stay at home and help their mothers and the remainder of their time is studying. They are kept under strict discipline, and this helps produce good results with their studies.

My Daughter is My Son

It is commonly said by fathers to a daughter that she is his son. Not all daughters have the privilege of being called the father's son. Only a daughter who is hardworking and helps her father in family matters will be called his son.

Although she remains a daughter and a female, she enjoys the status of her brothers.

However, she is still under family rules. If she needs to go to the fields, she cannot go alone, as her brothers go, because the custom is that she needs to be accompanied by a male. She can be very hard working and brave, but going alone to the fields might be not safe for her. She is an honor for the family and so she must be protected by a male or an elderly female of the house.

Some young females who are educated, find employment and help to support the family enjoy the status of being a son in the family. If she needs to go to work alone, she will be allowed. However, she has to protect the respect and honor of the family by staying away from male company. If she has to work with males, she cannot have an intimate relationship with any male. She has to remember always that she is an honor to the family. A young woman without a boyfriend who is hard working and obedient to the family enjoys the status of being a son in the family.

Childless Women

Barren women have no identity. Only women able to deliver children have identity in Pakistani society. Therefore, women unable to bear children stand nowhere. They are not recognized as being complete. This is considered unfortunate and unlucky and not worthy of her being in the family. She is abused throughout her life.

Pregnant women must avoid any interaction or contact with her. For example, if a childless woman visits a house where a woman lives who is pregnant or wishes to be pregnant, the latter must avoid any contact her. Furthermore, it is believed that if a visiting childless woman showers at the house, all her evil will be transferred to a young married woman of the house. Therefore, people do not allow childless women to shower in their homes. However, it is a common practice in Pakistan that if someone visits the house and is known well by the family, that person can shower.

Childless women suffer emotional pain. They give much money to those whom they think can restore their fertility with magical powers. Usually, this attempt does not restore fertility, but monetarily much is taken from innocent Pakistani women.

Shadow of Childless Women

It is believed that the shadow of childless women is dangerous and to be avoided because it can affect the fertility of young women.

Single Mothers

There are divorced women and widows but no single mothers in Pakistan. Having a child without a marriage or before a marriage is unforgivable. She has no right to live in society. It is an insult to the family.

Daughters-in-law

Internally, a daughter-in-law does not accept the bossing of her mother-in-law. She wants to live her life, but she cannot, because there is no life for her other than obeying her mother-in-law's wishes. She has to learn to develop skills for adjusting to her new home even though some aspects of her new life do not make sense to her.

She must accept this and suffer in silence because she wants to retain the respect of her parents. Furthermore, an agitated daughter-in-law is not acceptable. She has to learn to be silent and obedient, and these two skills are the most important skills she must learn. The more silent, the more successful a daughter-in-law becomes.

A majority of daughters-in-law compromise and choose to be silent, but some will take a stand and this diminishes respect for her as well as for her parents who will feel insulted because she has not kept her marriage vows. A daughter-in-law who who breaks her silence face separation or divorce. She can return to her parents and remain with them. Women who do not take a stand against living miserably in a new household will all their lives struggle with the dilemma that has brought them much silent suffering.

At the death of their husbands, a small number of women will remarry but the majority will stay with their parents as widows. Culturally, it is more acceptable to remain a widow than to enter a new marriage.

Women and Shrines

Pakistani women do not enjoy a social life. There are no opportunities for them to enjoy recreational opportunities outside the house. If married, they remain at home or go to the home of their parents where they are expected to only cook and work. Culturally, they are not allowed to leave the house alone for an outing and fun because it is believed there is no security for them outside the four walls of their house.

The safest place for women to go is to shrines. Christian women go to church or to Christian shrines to socialize and Muslim women go to shrines for praying and as an outing. Their families understand and will agree to take them to a church or to a shrine, but most will not agree to take women for outings because it is not safe and culturally it is not good for the family's reputation to take their women out often. With this in mind, women who want to go out will demand to be taken to a shrine where they can give their devotions and at the same time have access to some socializing.

Female Privacy

The concept of privacy is complicated. Women are considered private and they need to remain in privacy. Their presence in public places is not appreciated. However, there is no privacy in the family and everything is commonly used. If the family home is big enough, there is a sitting room for visitors waiting to see family members. Women visitors may enter other rooms to visit males and females whereas males who are not a part of the family remain in the sitting room.

Hope

Many Pakistani fathers hope that one day there will be peace and harmony so their daughters will be able to live a life of dignity and respect. Only education can bring change. Some change has come but more is needed.

Female Fertility Issues and Pakistani Behavior

If a Pakistani woman is unable to bear children, it means she is not healthy and she has to go to a doctor. Because it is strongly believed that a male cannot have any fertility issues, only she must go to the doctor. It would be shameful for him to go.

Sick Daughter-in-law

If a daughter-in-law becomes sick, the husband himself is considered unfortunate.

Sickness is considered unfortunate in the same way a sick daughter-in-law is considered unfortunate. As a result, a daughter-in-law will hide her sickness and suffer alone because she is afraid to talk about her sickness.

Life of a Widow

In Pakistan the life of a widow is full of challenges. Most young widows will leave their house and return to their parents or close family members. A majority of widows do not remarry because it is not considered respectable for a woman to remarry. She would be considered irresponsible. Some widows are supported by their in-laws but most are not supported. And so it becomes the responsibility of her parents to support her. If her parents are not living, her elder brothers become her support. She cannot survive alone and so she needs to be supported until her own children are ready to take that responsibility. If she has male children, there is little worry, but with daughters, she will feel burdened because of her obligations to raise and prepare marriages for her daughters. It is the responsibility of parents to provide dowries for them. Most widows are burdened with heavy loans after the marriages of their daughters, and these must be paid by the widow or her sons.

Bond of Parents and Children

A Pakistani relationship between parents and children is very strong and it is unbreakable. Parents support their children's educational, moral and financial needs as well as all other needs until their children begin working. Until then, children totally depend on their parents. Psychologically, when they begin working, the children feel and realize the responsibility and hardships of their parents. They vow to honor the sacrifices of their parents and to support their parents for all their needs.

Decision-Making and Children

In Pakistan, people normally do not make their own decisions. Parents make decisions for their children, and an extended families makes decisions for the extended family members. There are no free decisions; every decision has the influence of the family, which means an individual does not make the decision.

Children in a Male Dominated Pakistani Society

Children are considered a blessing to the family and they are raised with much love and care. A family without children is considered incomplete or without a blessing.

In Pakistan, a majority of women want to bear male children because this means she receives good care and respect from the family. If she bears a female child, the family normally accepts but not warmly. The father will desire that his wife have male children.

The process of raising a child is different for a male and female. Discrimination against female children begins at birth. A male child will enjoy favors and the best provisions for upbringing, but a female child's favors and advantages will be second best.

The mother is the last one to eat, and she eats the leftovers of her children. A female child will imitate the mother and feel proud to eat the leftovers of her brothers. This pride expresses her emotional attachment to them.

Male children are given the best care and are served better than female children because the males will always remain with the family. Females do not belong to the family once they are married and become part of another family. At the birth of a female child it is said she belongs to someone else. However, things are beginning to change because families are becoming more interested in educating their daughters in spite of opposition from some family members. Female children sometimes express anger for discriminatory treatment, but they are silenced by the family.

Pakistani children are raised with much physical and emotional care. They do not sleep alone but with their parents. Even if there are two children, they will sleep with their parents. The father sleeps in the same room but on a separate bed with one child and the other child is with the mother. When the children are grown, the father and male children will sleep in a courtyard and the girls will sleep inside the house with their mother on separate beds.

Children sleep a long time with their parents. Some male children sleep with their mothers until the age of thirteen, but eventually they must learn to sleep alone. Others sleep with their grandmothers or grandfathers.

Many male children continue to be breast-fed until the age of five because it is believed that children who are breast fed a long time are healthier. Mothers are emotionally more attached to their male children. Culturally, having more male children is a blessing and so mothers with more male children are considered very fortunate. They pay back their male children by taking good care of them because they have brought honor and respect to the family.

Children Raised at Home

Children in Pakistan do not go to childcare centers; they are cared for at home by their mothers or grandparents. Most women stay at home and raise their children while their husbands work to support the family.

For breakfast, children may be given bread with eggs, lentils or yogurt. They are not given tea, and instead, they will be given a glass of milk if it is available. Most poor families cannot afford milk and butter, and so their regular breakfast consists of bread and a cup of tea. For lunch, it is common to have bread with a mango, green chili pickle, green onions and mint. Dinner can be vegetables, such as baby pumpkin, and lentils or eggs.

A majority of children in Pakistan do not have toys. When they play outside, they play with Nature and they make toys with clay. They will climb trees.

Child Responsibility

Children legally become adults at the age of eighteen, but culturally they are not considered as adults until they are employed and bring in income. As mentioned earlier, they are supported by their parents until they can support their parents.

Birth of Twins

The birth of twins is a blessing in Pakistan to some extent. A woman giving birth to twin males would be considered a very fortunate woman. If she delivers male and female twins, she is not that fortunate but she is still fortunate. If she delivers two females, she would be considered lucky only if earlier she has delivered some male children for the family. For example, if there are four or five male children and she delivers female twins, this is lucky because the family needs females and she has fulfilled a need. But, if the family does not have male children and has only females, this is not fortunate for the family or for the mother. In order to gain some respect, a woman should have male children. Women with a number of male children boast among women because it is a blessing that contributes to the social and political status of the family. The more males, the more powerful is the family.

At the birth of male twins, tree branches are hung at the entrance to the house to announce that the family has been blessed with two male children.

Sometimes a woman who delivers female children is abused by her husband or her in-laws. These women are often divorced because they have not been able to bear male children for the family.

Child Adoptions

Child adoptions are not common and if there is an adoption taking place, this will often be a verbal contract. It is not a legal process, but families respect this. In a majority of cases, children are not told about their real parents. It is kept secret.

When adopted children hear about their real parents from others, in some cases they return to their real parents. Foster parents do not encourage frequent interaction between their adopted children and the real parents and this becomes confusing for the children.

Adoptions are generally done within the family or extended family. Giving up children for adoption is shameful, and that is why people are hesitant to do this.

Parents who give up their children for adoption do not enjoy respect in society.

Culturally, they would be considered irresponsible because they have been blessed with children and so giving up the children shows they are unable to take the responsibility.

Most parents prefer to adopt male children because male children will eventually take care of their parents. Female adoption is avoided because female children are considered expensive. Once they become adults, they must be married, which means parents must give a dowry. This is impossible for many parents due to poverty.

Disabled children are neither adopted nor given for adoption. Culturally, people are not willing to adopt a disabled child because a disability is considered a curse. Also, parents are not willing to give their disabled children for adoption because of embarrassment.

Eye Contact

Males reaching their teens are discouraged from having eye contact with females who have reached their teens. Likewise, these females are not allowed to have eye contact while talking with male teenagers. This is shameful for the female's family, but not for male's family.

Because this cultural restriction is imposed on females, they are hindered from developing self-confidence. They learn not to face males and they find it difficult to work with males. They remain powerless in a male-dominated society.

After eighteen, eye contact with males is strictly forbidden, and women have to obey this by all means. They are repeatedly taught and reminded by female elders not to look at a male. Women will even cover their faces when talking to a father-in-law.

Eye contact with her parents and brothers is allowed, but to look into the eyes of an elder means she is challenging the family and challenge is unacceptable. If a female is scolded, she must keep her eyes down, and if she dares to look at the person who is scolding her, she will be warned to keep her eyes down.

Men cannot have eye contact with women. Looking into their eyes is disrespectful. Men cannot look into the eyes of their male elders when talking to them because this is disrespectful.

If You Play with Girls, You Will Get Pimples on Your Ears

Pakistani children are born without racial and social discrimination. Yet, they are brought up with tribal and primitive customs in such a manner that they are segregated on all basic issues. Male and female children are discouraged from mingling and playing with each other. When I was a child, my mother always scolded me not to mingle with girls. She would use all her techniques to keep me away from them and from playing with them. She would tell me that if I play with girls, I will get pimples on my ears. As a child, this frightened me, and I would run away when I saw girls calling me to play with them.

Good-Looking Children

When children are born and they are beautiful, their foreheads will be marked with black to protect them from bad looks and bad thoughts.

Female Children and the Neem Tree

Culturally, it is believed that female children grow like the fast-growing neem tree (Dhraik tree).

Children and Science

Pakistani children who have attended school through the eighth grade begin high school. The majority have parents who encourage them to study science because it is thought that studying science will bring good jobs at schools or scientific institutions. Children tend to be impressed by their science teachers who receive respect and honor at the school. However, children studying science whose minds have low scientific interest tend to be unsuccessful with their studies.

Marriages Unite Families

A majority of marriages are arranged without the consent of the children. It is the mother or father or family members who must like the person their son or daughter will marry. When marriages are arranged, it takes sometimes months to come to a final decision because there is so much discussion and consultation in the family about the proposal. Surprisingly, the person for whom the decision is being made is often ignorant of the proposal. Depending on circumstances, sometimes a decision is made immediately,

Love Marriages

A small number of marriages involve the consent of the parties and the parents. The children may share their likes and dislikes and then accordingly, a decision is made while keeping in mind the will of the parties. If there is an understanding and willingness, then, in most cases the family may agree, but sometimes, in spite of the consent of the parties, a family may oppose the marriage and never allow it to take place.

Marriage without Parental Permission

Although most marriages are arranged by consenting parents, a small number of marriages are made against the will of the parents. These are arranged secretly. Due to social pressure and potential serious consequences, if a marriage does not have the consent of parents, the newly weds must live far from them because the parents will be tough on their female child who, they believe, is giving a bad example to the family and to society. A boycott can be put into place and the female will not be allowed to enter the house of her parents.

Boycott

In Pakistan, a person who is boycotted is supposed to leave the village. Sometimes his head, mustache, and beard are shaved. Sometimes the whole family must leave. Boycotts only take place because of issues of disrespect. For example, if someone is involved in abduction and rape of a woman, this can lead to a boycott. Fortunately, such occurrences do not happen often and so boycotts do not take place often.

Relationship of Sons to Their Parents after Marriage

After marriage, the relationship of a son to parents can weaken. A married son must begin to give his attention and support to his new family, and this makes the parents suffer because they expect continued attention and support. The behavior of the son brings psychological pain to the parents, and it is also a sign of shame for them. Some sons, in order to avoid shame, try to give their attention and support to their new family and their parents, and this is often not smooth.

Remaining Single

Remaining single in Pakistani is not a choice. Culturally, it is expected that every child is married because that is the goal of the parents. If a child does not want to marry and intends to remain single, there can be a forced marriage. Often, girls marry against their will, and sometimes a girl will never marry because her family does not want her to marry. Or, girls do not marry because their brothers do not wish this, which means they remain unmarried by force. They are not expected to express their desire.

Few families will support a choice of their daughter to remain unmarried. Culturally, this is a sign of disrespect for the family and for the one who remains single.

Dating

For fear that family members will catch them, those who date must do it in a hurry.

Dating is not culturally approved. However, dating does take place in secret. The parties are trying to understand each other. A majority of secret visits are more emotional than logical.

Kissing

Kissing in public is forbidden and unacceptable, unlike Western societies where kissing publicly after a wedding validates the marriage. In Pakistan, kissing a wife publicly is shameful and disrespectful. It is not only a shame and disrespectful to a bride and bridegroom, but also it is disrespectful to both the families and to everyone present. The parents, grandparents, and elders kiss their children and grandchildren. If someone is seen kissing in public, even a girlfriend, the gesture could instigate a beating.

CHAPTER 2

PHYSICAL CHARACTERISTICS
AND PREFERENCES

Short Height

Culturally, a short person is not admired and is given derogatory names. Females do not like to be married to a short male and a short female is not admired. To be short and also dark-skinned is a liability.

Tall Male, Wisdom and Ankle

A common saying in Pakistan is that a tall man's wisdom is not in his head but in his ankles. Because he does not use his brain, he is not intelligent. Ankles in the body are the wrong place for intelligence, and so a tall man is not very intelligent.

Wisdom and Pakistani Women

It is commonly said in Pakistan that a foolish woman's wisdom is not in her head but in her bun, and that is why she is unable to use her brain.

White Hair and Wisdom

White hair is a sign of wisdom. People who are old and have white hair are considered to be wise, but if they are not, it said that there is white hair but no wisdom.

Monkey Symbolizes Ugliness

The word monkey is used to describe an ugly person. Some parents and elders call their children or youth monkeys, but this is not taken seriously because of respect for parents and elders.

Long Hair and Males

Male children and youth like long or medium length hair. Musicians like long hair. Elderly males like their hair short.

Long Hair and Pakistani Women

Long hair is a sign of respect and honor for a Pakistani woman. If she does not have long hair, it means she has nothing, and it also means she is nothing. Hair cut to resemble a boy's cut is not liked.

Hair Cutting

In separate shops, males have their hair cut by males and females have their hair cut by females. There is no mixing of gender.

Bald Head and Wealth

A male who has a bald head is supposed to be wealthy, and so, when someone is losing hair, it means he will be rich. This consideration is only for men and not for women.

Beard

Culturally, the beard used to be a sign of respect and a good reputation.

Mustache

A person with a mustache is considered a man, and if he does not have one, he is considered as nothing. Furthermore, without a mustache, he is considered as being not trustworthy.

Dark Skin

Historically, early people living on the subcontinent of India were dark skinned and they came from the civilizations of Harappa and Mohenjo-daro. Then the arrival of Greeks, Arabs and Mughals brought white skin to the subcontinent and there was intermarriage.

Presently, black skin is not popular in Pakistan. Although families admire their dark-skinned son or daughter, they will not admire others for having dark skin. They would like to marry their dark-skinned son a white-skinned female, but they would not want their white-skinned daughter to marry a dark-skinned male.

Brown Skin

A majority of people in the provinces of Punjab and Sind have brown skin, and this color is attractive in Pakistan but not as attractive as white skin.

White Skin

White is considered a beautiful color in Pakistan, and people with white skin are liked and admired. Those with white skin feel proud. Parents arranging marriages for their children will look for white-skinned candidates.

Mole on the Heel

A mole on the heel means the person is a traveler. People will say he cannot stay home; he is always out; he does not like to be home; he is always on his feet and the mole does not let him sit.

Mole on the Cheek

A mole on the cheek of a girl is a sign of beauty.

Mole on the Lips

A mole on the lips indicates a talkative person, and so, when one sees a mole on the lips, that person is assumed to be very talkative. This assumption is common among the rural and traditional tribes of Pakistan.

Black Mark on the Tongue of a Pakistani Woman

A black mark on the tongue of a Pakistani woman is considered unfortunate. This mark would be considered unlucky. She would have to be careful when speaking in order not to reveal the black mark on her tongue. Because it cannot be surgically removed, she remains unfortunate throughout her life.

Ear Piercing

Ear piercing of women is common. Some tribes have a tradition of piercing the ears of male children, and some male adults pierce their ears. Most ears of females are pierced during their childhood, although some have them pierced when they are a bit older. Girls who have their ears pierced during childhood usually belong to families who like to gift earrings and even nose pins to their daughters and granddaughters.

Nose Pins

Some women like to wear nose pins, but mostly they are worn by brides and young women at weddings. Nomadic women always wear them.

Wealth and Wisdom

Culturally, it is believed that wealth makes one wise, and so, even mentally retarded members of a wealthy family are considered wise.

CHAPTER 3

INDIVIDUAL BEHAVIOR

Letting Go

Pakistani parents and elders teach children that the key to success is letting go. When girls are married that is the first advice given to them and they must act upon this advice. When young men are moving to other places or getting married, parents give them the same advice. In order to be successful, one must know the art of letting go.

Understanding Tolerance

The people of Pakistan are tolerant. Their daily life begins and ends with tolerance, and they are ready to tolerate culturally. Along with the concept of tolerance is the idea of 'letting go' as part of their lives. They can tolerate because they know how to let things go.

Understanding Shame

Shame is a respectful gesture, feeling and attitude that helps protect from disrespect. It also keeps one aware of the respect of others. When people say 'shame on you', this means to look into one's self to be aware of what one is doing. If someone does a shameful act, it is considered that he has not used his sense of shame. Feelings of shame keep one aware of everything around one's self.

Fear of Society

In Pakistan, people feel they must please society even though no attention is given to the ability to afford this. For example, Pakistanis feel they must give a dowry for their daughter at the time of marriage even though they may not be able to afford it. They do it because they want to earn respect from society.

Stubbornness

Stubbornness is considered a bad attitude and it is not appreciated. Children are discouraged and even punished for stubbornness. Even though stubborn children are difficult to handle, they are never taken to counselors. Parents handle the matter in their own way. Stubborn adults are considered dangerous because their stubbornness can make trouble for the family and friends. In general, people are afraid of the stubborn and their company is avoided. Family pressure is the only way to deal with stubbornness.

Verbal Abuse

Verbal abuse is common in Pakistan and little is done to stop it. Due to a lack of awareness, people do not have access to the courts, and there is also little trust in courts. People tend to prefer to deal personally with matters rather than going to court. The poor are the most verbally abused in Pakistan. The wealthy hold political and economic powers which means they control everything. Culturally, the one who is powerful can stop the verbal abuse but the weak cannot because of weakness.

Screaming

Screaming is common in Pakistan. Teachers scream at students and business owners scream at employees. Nurses scream at patients and even at visitors and families. Parents scream at their children.

Swearing

Swearing is not an acceptable practice in Pakistan. Respectable people prefer not to swear. Additionally, they want to be faithful to their word and to keep their promises.

Hooting

Hooting at schoolmates is common among students attending all levels of schools, but they do not hoot during educational and recreational programs. Hooting is also common among political parties, although it is usually not tolerated during serious disputes or disagreements.

Shoes, Symbol of Disrespect

The shoes is a symbol of disrespect and that is why beating with shoes is total disrespect because it indicates the person being beaten does not exist and is not worthy of any respect.

Understanding Defeat

Pakistanis understand, appreciate and support a winner, but it is difficult for them to understand defeat. A defeated one is considered of no use. Families have the same attitude toward their children, and so, the children learn that in order to receive appreciation, they must win by any and all means in order to avoid rejection. This fear of rejection is carried with them throughout their lives.

Understanding Honesty

Pakistanis understand that honesty means being faithful, and a person who is honest is actually called a faithful person. They believe that every value flows from one's faith, and honesty is the fruit of faithfulness.

Understanding Peace

The concept of Peace should come from within, and yet, the majority of Pakistani are struggling to find peace outside themselves. Generally, it is believed that peace within Pakistan does not depend on personal action, and that is why there is a personal struggle to find peace elsewhere. In search of this, people are ready to migrate and many are migrating to foreign countries.

The Concept of Simplicity

In Pakistan, a simple person is not showy and he lives a private life. He is not interested in his surroundings, nor does he want to benefit or harm anyone. He lives in his own world. Usually, simplicity is understood and mixed with the concept of untidiness, which means an untidy person is also considered simple.

CHAPTER 4

SOCIAL BEHAVIOR

Understanding of Diversity

Traditionally, Pakistan has been a diverse society, and people have been used to being tolerant of diversity. There has been much interaction among different groups, and tribes and clans have worked together and come to each other's aid when needed. Now, today, the sense of diversity has weakened and it needs to be strengthened so tolerance can return. Always, cultural festivals such as kite flying and celebrations of harvesting have been enjoyed with a sense of diversity, and this needs to be returned.

Friendship

In Pakistan, friendship is a sacred relationship and a friend becomes a part of the family as a brother. He is expected to be faithful, trusted and reliable, and he is to be available during times of sorrow and happiness. He may be absent during a time of happiness but he cannot skip his participation in times of sorrow. His presence plays an important role and this gives support to the family.

Concept of Visitation

Visits are very common in Pakistan. People love to visit their friends, relatives and their loved ones. A majority of visits are not scheduled, and it is considered more welcoming if your loved one comes without notice. Among the lower and lower middle classes, unscheduled visits are a routine. The protocol of giving respect and care is the same for uninvited and invited guests.

Neighbor visits are common and these visits can be extended throughout the day. Some visits are business related and some are for chatting, but most are for fun and entertainment.

Visits are common in the evening during the summer and during the winter, the best time is in the afternoon. Those who work go out-of-town to visit for two or three days, and if they do not work, visits may extend to more than a week. No appointment is necessary for visiting, but advance notice brings good treatment and attention. A common practice in Pakistan is to bring a gift, such as fruit. Those being visited will be offered something to eat, and it is best to accept because requesting will continue. Shoes are to be taken off, and because most families do not have couches, they will offer a bed to sit on. To use a bed for sitting means the guest has become part of the family.

Garlands and Guests

People love to garland their loved ones with flowers and money. The most valuable guests—religious, political, foreigners—are welcomed with garlands of money because garlands of money are considered more valuable than garlands of flowers. If a guest is not that important, he will only be welcomed with a garland of flowers. Usually, children will offer garlands to guests, and they will also welcome guests with a hug and a kiss.

Oil Pouring Welcome

A common custom in Pakistan when someone of importance comes to the house is for a women to stand at the door and pour oil at the entrance just before the guest enters the house. This custom is to show deep respect for the guest, and it is also a way to express love and respect from the entire family to the guest coming to their house.

Offering a Glass of Water

Offering a glass of water to a visitor is very important. As soon as friends or relatives enter the house, they are offered a glass of water. Soda and other cold drinks are offered to important guests (employer, in-laws, and others). If a glass of water is not offered, it is considered an insult to a visitor. It would be considered more respectful if a glass of water is offered by a woman. If a visitor refuses, an offer will continue, and so it is best for a visitor to put a glass of water in front of him so he can drink it when he wants.

When a Pakistani is in the hospital and a family visits, if food cannot be given to the visitors, then an offer of a glass of water upon their arrival would be very much appreciated.

Paying Guests

There is no concept of a paying guest in Pakistan. Culturally, it would be embarrassing for the family. They will not accept formal payments, but the guest can find a discrete way to pay the family.

Preparing Dough and a Guest

While preparing dough, if flour jumps on the counter, this means a guest is coming to the house. The woman preparing the flour will pray for a good, unexpected guest.

Visiting Small Houses

Pakistani houses usually have one or two rooms. Village homes may have only one room with a large courtyard. Every room is a bedroom. There is no office or dining room. Most normal living is done on beds that act as chairs. Wherever a bed is, it is used for visitations, eating, sleeping, and relaxing. School children use beds to do their homework.

Neighbors

Having a good neighbor is a sign of blessing. People enjoy and love to develop good friendly relationships with them. Elders spend their time talking to their neighbors. When a farmer harvests first fruit, it is shared with his neighbor.

When children are home alone, it is the neighbor who takes care of them during the absence of their parents. Neighborhood women are called aunts and neighborhood men are called uncles to the children of absent parents. In villages, the concept of neighborliness is very strong but it is weakening in cities. Due to terrorism, people are losing trust and this eventually leads them to distrust.

Prayer

Businesses, contracts and deals are run with prayer. Everything that is done begins and closes with prayer. There is a belief in the power of prayer. Prayers are said for the sick and for solved and unsolved issues.

Children's Prayers are Heard

It is believed that the prayers of children are heard and therefore children are asked to pray for the granting of what is needed.

Expressing Thankfulness

Being thankful, expressed in different ways, is an important part of daily life in Pakistan. The first fruit from a farm is presented at a worship place in order to be thankful for the protection of the crop. Another way to express thankfulness is to distribute food among the poor. Some take food to orphanages and to the homes of the elderly.

Expressing Joy

Joy is expressed in various ways. On happy occasions, cooked sweet rice is distributed among the people or it is donated to a place of worship or at a shrine. Another way to express joy or happiness is to dance to the rhythm of a drum. A professional drummer is invited to play so that dancing for joy can be expressed. A third way to express joy is the act of eating together either with the family or at a community level.

Laughing

Laughter is enjoyed by everyone, and so, Pakistanis like to go to comedy shows. There is no restriction on laughing itself, but there are restrictions on how women laugh. They are not to laugh outside the house, and even in the house, a female cannot laugh loudly when male elders are home because that is considered disrespectful. A male has no restrictions.

Listening

Listening in Pakistan is understood differently from the western world. In Pakistan listening means listening only. There are no questions. Asking questions would be understood as a challenge and disobedience, especially when the young are listening to an elder.

Communication

Most communication in Pakistan is now by land telephone or cell phone, which has replaced letter writing. Because Pakistani villagers have no computer or e-mail access, they depend on land phones or cell phones. Phoning is expensive but Pakistanis like to talk instead of writing. In the cities, e-mail is the most reliable source for communication.

Pakistani Greeting

Pakistanis love to greet and every day begins with greetings. Children proudly greet parents, grandparents and elders. Every elder is to be greeted. Only one word is used to greet—Salam or Asalam-0-Alakum. Asalam-O-Alakam is the Arabic greeting.

Being Alone

Pakistanis do not like being alone: they prefer to be with others. Commonly, meals are not eaten alone because this is considered not a healthy sign. If someone is eating alone, he will invite someone to join him. The tendency is to believe that those who live alone are not normal. One has to belong somewhere. Those who live with their families are considered respectable. Close relatives prefer to sleep in the same room and they enjoy chatting with each other while in bed and going to sleep. It is not a custom for people to travel alone, and now, for security reasons, people very much want to travel with others. They will travel with a friend or with family members. When women travel, they must have family members travel with them.

Social Support Groups

There are no groups in Pakistan that provide social support. People do not like to talk about their social issues in groups. Sharing social issues in a group is considered disrespectful.

Volunteering

The concept of volunteering is as old as the history of the subcontinent. Pakistanis understand the importance of volunteering at shrines and religious centers because volunteering at sacred places brings blessings for the family. Otherwise, the concept of volunteering is weak.

Empathy

Pakistanis are very empathetic during happy and difficult times. It is considered an obligation to visit the sick to express empathy to a grieving person or family. It is out of question to be unable to be with someone experiencing a difficult time. One's presence is enough to express feelings of empathy.

To be present at a celebration is very important but not as important as being present during difficult moments of life.

Sympathy

Pakistanis are very sympathetic. They express their sympathy by talking with suffering individuals and families. Instead of listening to a sick person they will take matters in to their own hands by suggesting natural treatments without having knowledge and experience of what they are talking about.

Complaints

Pakistanis do not like to complain about social matters. For example, they will endure no electricity for weeks and not complain. One reason for not complaining is that they know little attention is paid to complaints given to authorities.

However, complaints are voiced if they concern a tribe or family threatened with a loss of dignity. For example, if there is trash in the streets, no one will complain, but if trash is thrown into their homes, they will be ready to complain and they will speak with their family elders.

Forgiveness

The concept of forgiveness is not strong. A person who forgives is considered weak because it does not bring power. Thus, the act of revenge takes place so the person can be considered powerful.

A woman is the honor of a family and if someone robs her respect, this is unforgivable. Robbing her respect is similar to raping her. Tribes and communities can fight for decades and centuries in revenge for the robbing of a woman's respect.

Poor people may be forced by the powerful to forgive, but the powerful must use revenge to maintain their power. If power is challenged, this also becomes unforgivable.

Forgiveness is also a sign of shame, and so, to not seek revenge is a shame to society. However, forgiveness in Pakistan can be seen among children who play and fight every day because they forgive each other and return to playing together.

Pakistani women are more forgiving than men, and they can be ready to negotiate and talk, but it is very difficult to persuade a Pakistani male to forgive. There can be forgiveness for a male's action, but not for a woman's action. For example, if a woman develops a relationship with a male, her punishment is death because she has not respected the family. There is no dialogue on this type of issue.

Nepotism

Nepotism is common in Pakistan and it is preferred that a family member inherits political and social responsibilities of the family. People bribe in order to secure undeserved favors for their relatives. There is no solution to this and society continues to live with nepotism.

Standing In Line

Once in Pakistan, I was standing in line at a booking office and an elderly man broke into the line and bought his ticket from the reservation clerk. It would seem that he had violated all rules, but the reservation clerk said nothing and issued his ticket. No one was agitated. In Pakistan, rules were violated because influential people were standing in line. The custom is to send their employees to stand in all types of weather, the heat of the sun and the cold of the winter. The elder, the oldest, trumps power.

Questions

Questions are not encouraged in Pakistan. The one who asks many questions is not considered a good person, and so, in order to be good, one has to be silent. Most doctors in Pakistan do not like to respond to the questions of their patients. When people ask them questions, they ignore this and remain silent. The same attitude can be found under most circumstances in Pakistan.

Pleasing Society

In Pakistan, people feel they must please society even though no attention is given to the ability to afford this. For example, Pakistanis feel they must give a dowry for their daughter at the time of marriage even though they may not be able to afford it. They do it because they want to earn respect from society.

Blessings

Throughout Pakistan the concept of blessing is strong. Butter is a sign of blessing and needs to be well cared for and shown respect. When there is an abundance of butter in the home, this is also an abundance of blessing. Milk is a blessing and the abundance of milk indicates an abundance blessing. It is shared in places of worship and it is also presented in the home to guests. It is carefully regarded so it is not wasted. Wasting milk is wasting blessing. Families who do not take care of milk are not considered wise.

Daily Living and Spirituality

Spirituality of Pakistan is not separate from daily life. Every action taken in the family or outside the family is part of spirituality. It is the sacred responsibility of the mother to provide care for the family, and it is also a sacred responsibility of the father to provide care for the family. No one can escape sacred responsibility. Duties have to be fulfilled. During difficult times, the family does not go to counselors for advice. Instead, they go to family elders who give guidance for restoring spiritual energy. Offering a glass of water in itself is a spiritual act. Meals are eaten together, and this is part of a spiritual exercise.

Spirituality of Animals

It is believed that animals are a blessing and therefore animals are well cared for. Milk-giving animals are treated well. They bring prosperity to the family, and so every family member serves and looks after them with attention and care. Animals that do not give milk are also a blessing because through them, the house business is run and managed.

Feeding Water Creatures a Blessing

Some people go to the rivers or canals to throw food to the water creatures. This is considered a good act and it is done to gain the prayers of the water creatures.

Feeding Ants a Blessing

Ants are considered a blessing and some people feed them by throwing grain in ant holes so they can eat. Their presence is considered a blessing. However, some people who do not believe this will kill them with chemicals.

Eye Pulsation

Pulsation in the right eye is considered an omen of a desirable coming event, whereas pulsation in the left eye is considered unlucky and something unfortunate will happen to an individual or someone in the family.

Right Palm Itch

An itch in the right palm means he/she or someone in the family will receive money.

If the itch is strong, the expectation becomes stronger.

Left Palm Itch

If someone feels an itch in the left palm, it means he/she will lose money.

First Tooth

If the upper teeth of a child come first, this is not a good sign, and so the maternal grandfather will come and push them back with a bronze vessel. It is very painful for the little child, but this must be done to save the family and the child from any unpleasant events.

Teeth Grinding

When people grind teeth while sleeping it is considered an omen, and so teeth grinding is considered normal and no one is taken to the doctor for treatment. Teeth grinding is not a good sign because it means that something unusual or unpleasant is expected.

Sneezing

When one sneezes, it means someone is missing or remembering you at that particular moment.

Spitting and Saving from Bad Eye

When someone in the family is beautiful and attractive, family members spit symbolically at the person in order to save him from bad looks that can affect him. If someone is beautiful and becomes sick after a lot of praise, this means that this person has been affected by the bad looks of the people.

Spitting a Sign of Rejection

In order to express extreme hatred in disputes, people will spit. This also means there is no relationship and this relationship cannot be restored. There is a complete boycott.

Spitting on Face and Moles

Children who spit on the faces of others are warned by their mothers that those who spit will have moles growing on their faces, and so children are scared to spit.

Touching Gums with Tongue

At the age of seven, when baby teeth begin to fall out, children wait for new teeth to come in. During this waiting period, children begin touching their gums with their tongues to feel the new teeth growing. Mothers discourage this practice of touching by warning that the new teeth will grow in crooked and be weak. Some children are scared, but those who are not scared may tease their mothers by touching their gums with their tongues.

Jewelry, a Sign of Respect

Jewelry is sign of respect and it indicates prosperity.

Artificial Jewelry, a Sign of Poverty

Women who do not have gold jewelry are considered poor. This lack of gold jewelry indicates that she is not rich and she is not looked after by her husband and in-laws.

Parrot Astrologer

Parrot astrologers are on the streets of Pakistan to entice people into paying for a prediction of their future by picking a lucky card.

Fake Palmists on the Pavements

Hundreds of fake palmists are on the pavements of Pakistani cities to fool the uneducated class by predicting their future. They charge much money to give these innocent people false hopes.

Gift Sharing

Gift sharing at religious and social festivals is very important. Most gifts are in the form of cloth, toys, and so forth, and these are shared with family members. It is very necessary to give gifts within the family. Otherwise, there could be serious anger among one another that can stop communication for months. That is why it is a powerful custom at festival time to share gifts within the family.

Pakistanis Think with the Heart

The simple, uneducated people of Pakistan feel and think with their hearts. They look for leaders who can think and feel the same way, and they find the majority are not this way. They look for leaders who can feel the pain and suffering they feel.

CHAPTER 5

EDUCATION

Value of Education

In a typical Pakistani family not all children go to school, although most prefer to have their sons educated but not their daughters. Sons are an asset to the family and its identity, and this is a good reason to educate them. Daughters do not belong to the family because eventually they will be married and become part of the family of her in-laws. Therefore, her education would not benefit the family. Teenaged girls are stopped from going to school. A small percentage of Pakistani families understand a value in treating their male and female children equally.

Children, both male and female, who become educated and financially successful, may take the responsibility of the whole family, which is not educated or financially viable. They make decisions for the family and they work hard to support it, sometimes putting their lives and even careers at risk to support a very large family that may include children of their siblings. This stress can give these caregivers emotional and physical problems.

Education and Pakistani Male Youth

Pakistani male youth are trained with much love, whereas girls are trained with strict rules. Because boys have recreational opportunities, they are not home most of the time. They are with their friends or at recreational centers. Due to their extra activities, they are unable to pay strong attention to their studies, and consequently their studies suffer. Now, however, there is a change and Pakistani male youth are becoming more serious about their educational issues.

Educated Male called Babu

An educated male in a family is called a babu, which means he is educated and therefore in a higher position than the uneducated.

Education and Jobs

Some parents ask themselves why they should have their child educated when there will be no jobs for their child. There is an understanding of the importance of education to achieve prosperity, but they do not trust that the system will allow the child to work after he is educated. Only a small number consider that education is a way to self-understanding.

English Medium Schools

The English medium school system was introduced by the British on the subcontinent of India. After independence in 1947, the system continued to educate the children of wealthy families. These schools never accepted children from the poor class, and they were established in areas where the wealthy live. This system continues to grow.

Urdu Medium Schools

There are Urdu medium schools in Pakistan on nearly every street of a town. These schools serve the poor children. Often Urdu medium schools do not have qualified staff and the teachers are poorly paid. In public schools there is no fee but privately owned Urdu schools charge a fee.

No Punjabi Medium Schools

There are no Punjabi medium schools, and Punjab is the only province in Pakistan that does not educate its Punjabi children in their native and mother tongue. Not only are they not taught Punjabi, they are discouraged to speak it even at home.

They are taught Urdu and educated in Urdu language. Punjabi is forbidden in educational institutions.

These children speak Urdu until they are teenagers, and then slowly they start speaking the Punjabi language. During their early childhood years, when they spoke Punjabi, they were scolded and discouraged by their parents because Punjabi is considered a language of the uneducated class. But these children, when they become adults, return to their mother tongue, and do not speak Urdu. They will speak Urdu when they are involved with business matters, but in all other matters Punjabi is spoken.

One Room Schools

One room schools are everywhere in Pakistan, even in poor communities. Students sit in unsanitary rooms with no furniture and with broken windows. These schools are not regularly inspected and those in charge do what they want. There is not enough staff to take care of the educational needs of the students. The teachers are hired because of political influence, and so it is difficult to have teachers transferred because of their political influence.

Floor (Tat) Schools

Tat schools for poor children have no furniture for sitting and so they bring their own piece of cloth for sitting on the floor. This education is affordable, but the system is very poor. Unqualified teachers are hired. These schools are cleaned by the children. In village schools there are no toilet facilities.

Tree Schools

Tree schools are generally in rural and undeveloped areas of Pakistan. During the summer, children receive an education under the shade of a tree, and in the winter they too sit under a tree in cold weather and wind. Most sit on the ground but some bring mats. There is one chair for the teacher, and it is considered respectable when a teacher can sit on a chair. Some teachers sit on a bed to teach and sometimes they lie on a bed and receive massages from the students. Massaging a teacher has been a traditional sign of respect but now it is no longer appreciated, although this style of teaching still exits.

Education and Disabled Children

In some areas of Pakistan, there are one or two educational centers available for disabled children, but in the majority of cities and villages there are no centers for them. The attitude is that disabled children are unable to learn with normal children and so there are no facilities for them. The majority of parents with disabled children do not have access to the few disabled educational centers, and as a result, these children are deprived of education and remain uneducated throughout their lives.

Studying Non-scientific Subjects

Studying non-scientific subjects is not considered wise. Children who choose to study art are not only considered unwise, but often they are teased by other students.

Half-year Exams

In Pakistan, the educational system has an exam called half-year exam which is taken after summer vacation. Children must prove how they have spent their time during summer holidays. Those who have studied well pass this exam and those who fail have not utilized their time well. Punjabi children call this exam 'Kachay Imtehan' (semifinal exams).

Annual Exams

In high school, annual exams are final exams. Punjabi children call them 'Pakay' exams. Students study for these exams day and night, and they ask their parents and relatives to pray for their success. The Pakistani examination system is so taxing, children have to learn everything by heart. They do not enjoy this and they would rather that these exams be eliminated.

Final Result Day in School

The final results for the school year are announced with much excitement by the students and their parents who have come to listen. The top three positions are announced by the principal and other results are announced by teachers in charge of classes. The children who gain first position bring sweets for the principal and their class teacher. Those who pass also bring sweets for their principal and teachers, and the latter are also garlanded. The children who fail are given advice by the principal. Some parents are happy with the results and others are not. The unhappy ones may request that the principal allow their failed children to advance to the next class, and this puts the principal in a difficult position because the requested favor is undeserved.

Sex Education

There is no sex education in Pakistan, and neither the parents nor society take the responsibility of educating children on this issue. Children receive this education through their own undependable means and they are misled. Culturally, talking about sex is not good. Therefore, no one talks about sex formally, but informally everything is discussed and shared. Because no one has scientific knowledge about sex, society has with many misconceptions.

Education and Children as Singers

Pakistani children are excellent singers and they love to sing and listen to music, which is part of a child's body and soul. They love education through music and singing, but unfortunately this is not encouraged.

Brick Factories and Education

Brick factory children do child labor, work under poor conditions, and they are deprived of education.

Tuition Centers

In Pakistan, tuition centers for learning after regular school hours have become an established business. Teachers have their own tuition centers and they recommend to their students that they attend these centers. Both good and poor students attend, and they must pay high fees to receive extra schooling at these centers.

Discipleship

Discipleship is a lifelong commitment because once a disciple, always a disciple. One cannot break this commitment: it has to be kept and respected. The commitment for discipleship is usually not a free choice. It is imposed by the family because of a family decision, and it must be respected because of family honor.

A student in school is actually in a discipleship with his teacher. He has been given by his parents to a teacher to make him into a human being or man. The teacher does the training with love, care and even sometimes given physical punishment. A disciple remains forever a disciple to his teacher or guru even when the teaching is completed. There is a requirement to continue the relationship, and so, each time a disciple comes to the teacher, he will offer a little gift to prove discipleship and respect. He even gives a massage to his teacher's legs as a show of respect for his teacher. This massage is also performed to prove that he is still a pupil of the teacher and in need of the teacher's blessing. In order to be a successful, good disciple, he needs the blessings of his teacher or guru.

CHAPTER 6

FOOD

Meat

Pakistanis love to eat meat, and they enjoy beef, chicken, mutton, and buffalo. Camel meat is also eaten, and rabbits are hunted for food. Mutton is expensive, and so, for those who can afford to buy mutton, it is usually eaten only twice a week. Beef is not as expensive as mutton.

Meat Eating and the Poor

Low income families in Pakistan cannot afford to eat meat, and therefore lentils and vegetables are part of their daily diet. They can only afford to enjoy eating meat once or twice a year.

Eating Fish

Fish is not a common food in Pakistan except along the coastal areas near the Arabian Sea. It is served at parties or eaten as a medical treatment. The poor rarely eat fish because it is too expensive to buy. In central and northern Pakistan, there are river and farm fish available. On riverbanks where caught fish are fried by fishermen, highway travelers are generally their customers. This fish is delicious, but after frying, if it is not covered, dust settles on it.

Fruit

Fruit is considered not as necessary to eat as bread, vegetables and meat. Therefore, it is eaten whenever it becomes available and it is enjoyed no matter what time of day.

Fruit Shopping

Buying fruit from a peddler is affordable, but good fruit is usually under a pile of fruit. And so, one is advised to dig deeply to find the best fruit. Usually, peddlers have good quality fruit, but one has to check all that is offered.

Watermelon

Watermelon is a summer fruit grown mostly in desert areas of Pakistan. It used to be economical. However, now it is not economical.

Male Children and the Mango

The mango is a slow-growing tree, and male children are compared to the mango tree when they grow slowly like the tree. It is common in Pakistan that male children are more often sick in their childhood than female children.

Tea

Tea is a popular, affordable drink in Pakistan. Mornings begin with a hot cup of tea and days end with tea. It is a sacred responsibility to offer tea to every visitor, and most guests do not refuse this offer. It is provided to the sick. If someone has a headache or stomach ache, tea is drunk as a medicine because it is believed that tea cures.

Milk and Butter

Milk and butter, mentioned earlier, are considered a blessing and therefore, they should be respected and never wasted. It is also expected that this blessing of milk and butter should be shared. If it is not shared, this is not a good sign.

Spice Eating

The people of Punjab and Sindh enjoy eating spices, and they add natural and manufactured spices to vegetable, lentil and meat cooking. Those living in the provinces of Pakhtoon Kha and Balochistan do not eat many spices, and yet, these foods are tasty and digestible. In Punjab, to cook tasty food, green peppers and red ground peppers are added excessively. Salt is also added excessively.

Red Chilies

Culturally, it is believed that excessive praise can cause physical or psychological pain and suffering. Therefore, if someone is sick because of exaggerated praise, this is considered the work of a bad eye. In order to get rid of a bad eye, mothers roll red chilies over the head of the one who has been affected.

Chickpeas

Pakistanis enjoy eating chickpeas fried in oil. Some enjoy them without gravy or curry and others enjoy them with gravy and curry. Rice is also boiled with them.

Chickpeas are a diet for horses and donkeys to keep them well nourished. This gives them energy to work

Corn (Chapati) Bread

Bread made from corn is popular in the corn growing areas of Pakistan. It is considered healthy to eat and people love to put butter on it. Guests are warmly presented with this corn bread specialty of the area.

Typical Lunch with Pickle

During the summer and most of the year a pickle is available in Pakistani homes to provide emergency food for unexpected guests. Guests in the cities will receive other food, but guests in the villages, if they arrive without advance announcement, are served a pickle and bread immediately.

Mustard Leaves and Spinach

When mustard leaves and spinach are cooked together, the mixture is called saag. Mothers love to cook these popular vegetables that are considered good for the digestive system. Often natural spices are added, and it is cooked mild or hot. Cooked with green chilies or ground red pepper means perspiring while eating. The mixture can be cooked with chicken, beef, or buffalo, and it is also popular to eat it with hot bread, called chapati, and fresh butter.

Almonds and Children

Children who are slow of speech and slow of tongue are given an antidote of almonds by their mothers. Some afflicted children are teased by their fellow children and the mothers want their children to be perfect.

Restaurant Waiters

Restaurant waiters generally are not treated well. They are mostly children employed by restaurant owners as cheap labor and they work long hours. They are not called by their name but rather, chotay, which means a kid.

Tip Giving

In a majority of restaurants, motels and hotels people love to give tips to the employees. These employees serve the guests well in order to receive good tips. Most guests give good tips, but sometimes, in spite of good service, guests do not give and this embarrasses the employees. It is very much appreciated if a good tip is always given.

CHAPTER 7

HEALTH

The Title of a Doctor

Unqualified individuals call themselves doctors in Pakistan and there is no control over this. A medical dispenser is also called a doctor, although this title is not recognized by the Pakistani government. Because socially and culturally they are recognized as doctors, people go to them for treatment even though they are not qualified.

Pakistani Woman and Medical Care

A Pakistani woman would prefer to be seen by female physicians because it is considered disrespectful if her body is seen and touched by male doctors. Her family also does not want to take her to male doctors. It is the family's choice and a final decision.

Healing Groups

Few Pakistanis are Christians, yet, many Christian healing groups have been formed to help heal anyone regardless of belief. Emphasis is on healing by prayer. They do not recommend medical or standard treatment. Those needing the healing often will undergo basic medical treatment first and then begin relying on prayer, which, in most cases, works.

Health Problems

A common attitude toward dealing with problems is to ignore them until they become overwhelmingly big. For example, a child complains about pain in her foot and the family ignores this and takes no action. The child continues suffering and still the family ignores her. Only when she can no longer walk and she falls to the ground with pain does the family take action. What has not been dealt with has become a big problem.

Managing Pain

Pakistanis suffer terribly when in pain and alone. For their physical pain, they prefer someone to be with them who will validate the pain. Most patients who are discharged after surgery recover better at home than in the hospital. The family provides support and help during pain, even though the family may be noisy. By talking and listening to the family, this helps the patient manage pain. Those who are left alone in physical pain may suffer both physically and emotionally, although, if there is emotional pain, Pakistanis will deny this. Instead, they will hide it. As a result of hiding emotional pain, it is not dealt with or resolved

Caregiver Support

Hospitals in Pakistan have religious leaders for patient care. They are not trained to be listeners and emotional caregivers. They provide prayers and readings, but there is little chatting with the patient and family and no emotional support is given. There is a great need for this.

Women and Hospitalization

When a woman needs to be hospitalized, she needs to be accompanied by at least one member of her family during hospitalization. This is because women are dependents, never left alone. To assume the role of independence is difficult for a woman to understand.

Cancer and Secrecy

Cancer is considered a fearful disease in Pakistan and it is not discussed with anyone who has been diagnosed with the disease. It is kept secret. A child with cancer is not told, and he will struggle to understand the anxiety of the family. Parents will take this child to different hospitals and specialists, but they will not share with the child who has cancer. Even if anxiety increases, no attention is paid to this issue. If the family instructs the doctor to hide the problem from the child, he will consent to do this.

Mental Health

Mental health issues in Pakistan are not discussed and are kept secret. A doctor may speak to a patient about mental health issues, but the family will avoid any discussion on mental health with their loved ones and outsiders. Culturally, it is believed that discussion on mental health issues will hurt the family and patient.

Headache

Headaches are common in Pakistan. It is believed that a headache caused by fatigue will go away with the passage of time. Interestingly, a majority of people with headaches will complain but not take pills. They may drink a hot cup of tea to ease the pain, but the complaining continues. Pills offered by a mother, grandmother, or wives are ignored unless the matter becomes serious.

Sun Shower

A sun shower in Pakistan is used extensively. During winter, people spend afternoons in the sun. They sit in the courtyard to chat, relax and enjoy tea or lunch. School children have their classes outside in the sun during the winter.

In Pakistan, summer is eight months, and so people have an opportunity to stay under the sun. They do not have to take vitamin D because they receive vitamin D from the sun. The sick sleep in the sun for warmth, and in village health centers, patients are laid in the sun.

Dry Skin and Oil

To keep dry skin moist, mustard oil is applied before or after showering. It is also applied to ears and the belly button, and it is mostly used by men.

Oiling the Hair

On weekends, men, women and children put mustard oil in their heads because they think the oil helps to keep their hair strong and healthy. Then they sit in the sun, which is a form of sun shower. The oil remains on the head for a couple hours and then a water shower is taken to remove it. Elder men use oil every day to keep their hair moist. Mothers keep the heads of their home-based children moist with mustard seed oil. A majority of women do not use it frequently.

Parasite Head Cleaning

To clean off lice and other insects, women pick each other's heads on weekends.

Flu and Cough

Flu and a cough are common in Pakistan during the winter months, but instead of going to the doctor, they treat themselves by eating boiled eggs or mixing them with a hot glass of milk. There is little education on flu and cough in Pakistan, and most do not take flu shots. They prefer alternative medicine which is affordable and approachable, or, they will wait until the disease goes away. They believe that Nature will heal them. Some elders use prayer to heal their flu and cough.

Licorice Root (Malathi) for Sore Throats and Coughs

Pakistanis use the juice of licorice root to cure sore throats and coughs. When it is chewed, the taste is sweet.

Sweet Jalebi and Milk for Treating a Cold

If someone catches a cold, he will mix Jalebi, a dessert, with milk and enjoy it. Having milk with Jailebi is energetic and it is often drunk after dinner. Most students like to drink this to keep their bodies energetic.

Black tea and Diarrhea

When people in Pakistan have diarrhea, they drink black tea with a banana. A Lipton tea bag or Lipton loose tea is used to prepare black tea.

Stomach Ache Remedies

A cup of tea is the first remedy for someone with a stomach ache. Some will add onions and mint to the tea. Also, a massage treatment will be given by a family member. When a stomach ache comes from eating spicy food, some will drink fresh, boiled cow milk.

Lasi, a Mixture of Water and Milk as a Blood Thinner

It is believed that Lasi keeps the body cool and it is also used as a blood thinner because it keeps the blood thin and the circulation flowing properly.

Burn Treatment

While cooking, if a woman receives a slight burn, she will not be able to apply any medicine or go to a doctor. She will ask her male children to pee on the burn to heal the skin.

Prickly Heat

Prickly heat, tiny red bumps on the skin, is common in Pakistan when the weather is dry from June to August. Pakistanis use powders to soothe it and this helps. In August, the weather becomes humid and prickly heat leaves.

Ear Care Remedy

If pain is felt in the ear, a traditional remedy is to add garlic to warm oil and when the oil is cooled a bit, it is put into the ear. A piece of cotton is then put in the ear.

This technique also heals pimples in the ear. Mothers teach their children not to put their fingers or anything else in their ears because the ears are a sensitive part of the body.

Traditional Eye Care

When the eyes are itchy, before going to a doctor, the tradition is to sprinkle cold/ice water on the eyes and that will begin healing the itchiness. It is the most common remedy for keeping the eyes clear and clean.

Tooth Care

For tooth care there is a natural method common to Pakistanis. After every meal, rinsing is done to keep the mouth clean. This not only protects the teeth but it cleans the mouth of odor. A majority of villagers use a toothbrush that is a small piece of a tree branch cut and chewed to make it soft. The soft side is used to clean the teeth. There is no need to buy paste because a natural paste is in the branch.

Massage

It is customary for family elders to enjoy a leg massage in the evening. Traditional massagers are not hired to do this because the family's children will give their elders a massage to help them sleep after a long day.

There are traditional, inexpensive massagers who will give a good massage at bus and train stations and other places.

Pregnant Women and Massage

As a means of therapy, before, during and after pregnancy a woman is given a massage by a traditional midwife who also councils and gives encouragement. She is not trained professionally, but she inherits her skill from her family. Today, midwives are being professionally trained to take care of pregnant women.

Cholera and the Watermelon

In order to avoid cholera, Pakistani people do not drink water after eating watermelon because it is believed that drinking water with or after eating watermelon causes cholera.

Natural Treatment for an Inability to Urinate

When Pakistanis experience urination blockage, they believe they can open the blockage by mixing a half cup of milk with water to make a drink called Lasi.

Also, to help urination difficulties, they will turn on the water tap to hear the flow of water when they are trying to urinate. If there is no water tap, another person uses a hand pump to pump water and the person with urination problems stays close in order to hear the sound of water, which can help ease the blockage problem.

Sore Mouth and Cow Milk

Sore mouths are treated with cow milk. To help heal, parents of children with sore mouths will take them to the cow and give them milk directly from the cow's teat.

Barley Drink

During the season of wheat harvest, barley drink is a popular drink with farmers because it is believed that barley is cold and thus it helps to keep the body cool during harvesting. Ground, cooked barley is put in water with brown sugar, mixed well, and then enjoyed. This inexpensive summer drink is sold by peddlers.

Dry Plums

Dry plums are dipped in water at night at room temperature and then water and plums are eaten the next morning. The juice and water keep the body cool during summer, and the drink helps to keep the digestive system working correctly.

Almonds and the Brain

Pakistani mothers keep almonds soaking in water all night and in the morning they are given to their children who are studying or doing mental work. It is believed that almonds keep the brain energetic and fresh.

Baby Pumpkin and Diabetes

Some people eat boiled baby pumpkin to keep their sugar level balanced. They also eat it when cooked with spices but normally people who really need to control their diet because of diabetes will eat boiled baby pumpkin without spices.

Bitter Melon and Diabetes

Bitter melon, taken as a natural medicine to treat diabetes, is either cooked or eaten as a salad. Although they are bitter, Pakistanis eat them to keep their sugar in balance.

Chickpeas and Diabetes

Pakistanis suffering from diabetes generously eat chickpeas to keep their sugar level balanced. Some eat chickpeas with bread.

Apple as Gold, Iron and Silver

It is said that eating an apple at breakfast is like eating gold, and at lunch like eating iron, and at dinner like eating silver.

Guava Good for Digestion

Guava, a common fruit in Pakistan during the winter, is eaten to support the digestive system. It is also one of the most affordable fruits of Pakistan, and it is available everywhere. One can even find peddlers selling them in the streets.

Street Dentists

Unqualified street dentists have small stalls with primitive equipment to treat all teeth problems with one remedy—removal of a tooth. The poor cannot afford to go to a qualified dentist, and so a street dentist is the only choice for them. After removal of a tooth, there is no follow up, and if there are complications, there is no treatment. Furthermore, street dentists claim no responsibility for their work.

CHAPTER 8

RURAL PAKISTAN

Agriculture

Seventy-five percent of Pakistanis are involved with agriculture. The majority inherit agricultural land, but females do not receive a share after distribution.

It is a sign of dishonor if one decides to sell agricultural land. He will be considered irresponsible and he will not be respected. Landowners have respect, and in order to keep this respect, he must retain the land.

The profession of agriculture is becoming so expensive that poor farmers cannot afford to buy seed and fertilizer. Because the belief in natural fertilizer has faded, farmers have been using expensive, imported fertilizers that they can no longer afford. Good loan programs are not available.

Male Farmers

Most farming is done by males. Male children who go to school help their farming parents after school hours, but they are not expected to learn farming techniques because it is thought that the educated do not farm. A male child who does not go to school works with his parents on the farm. Females do minor jobs in the fields, but their major work is to help feed the family.

Female Farmers

Although farming is usually not done by females, there are exceptions. If a family does not have male children, then it is the female who will take care of the family farm. She may hire male farmers to do major work but she will take care of everything else. Usually, watering agricultural lands is done at night and some women will do this with the help of a hired farmer. Animal care is also done by women.

Barefoot Farming

Many farmers feel uneasy wearing shoes when farming, and so most farming is done barefoot. They plow their fields barefoot, and they cut fodder for animals without wearing shoes. They water plants and crops barefoot.

Farming Starts Early

Farmers go to bed early and get up early because their day of work begins early.

They will work until 10 am when women from their house bring breakfast, which is usually a cup of tea and Lasi during the summer. In the winter, it is hot tea.

The men feed their animals, plow and dig in the fields. When it is dry, sometimes the fields must be watered the entire day or night. If there is night watering and women are helping, dinner is served inside the farmhouse before sunset so the women can safely return home before dark.

Usually, a farmer works in the fields all day and returns home in the evening after sunset. Then he enjoys food with his family and goes out for a walk with his friends, or he remains at home to chat with his family and go to bed.

He travels to a town or village to deal with shopping, banking, and any matter related to land or crops, such as buying fertilizer. He sells his farm products there.

If basic health matters require attention, he can receive this at most villages, but these health centers are not equipped to handle serious issues.

Farming with Machinery

Today most farming is done with machinery, such as a tractor, which is owned by someone in the village who will rent it at a high price to poor farmers. For this reason, most plowing is done on credit and the farmers pay when the crop is sold. Some of the payment may be a portion of the crop.

Grain Grinding

Every village and city has machinery for grinding grain that is then brought from the fields by donkey cart and bicycle, and some carry it on their heads and shoulders. The grain is weighed and then the farmers wait their turn for the grinding. They sit and chat with each other while they wait, and when the grain is ground, some pay cash and others pay by giving grain.

Shepherding

Shepherding is a common profession in Pakistan. Some herd goats and sheep and some herd buffalo. This is a profitable profession but demanding. Usually, a shepherd leaves with his animals in the morning, stays with them all day, and returns home at sunset. He takes his lunch with him and his herd rests and relaxes while he enjoys his lunch. Both men and women are shepherds and the majority are uneducated.

Villagers

A Pakistani village family generally consists of seven to nine members who live in a one or two room house. Usually the bathroom has a shower facility and toilet needs are handled in the fields.

Sometimes grandparents and unmarried maternal aunts begin living with the family and so the number of members is expanded. Family guests stay with them. Village families may have a big plot for their farming, but the house itself will have only one or two rooms.

If there is no electricity, summer afternoons and evenings are spent under a tree, and during the winter, afternoons are spent in the sun. All cooking, dish washing, other matters are done in the sun.

Power Crisis

Those villagers who have electricity must contend with daily power outages throughout Pakistan. Most villagers with electricity have it only for a few hours and then it is turned off. Cities are less affected by the power crisis. Residences of the wealthy often have generators to keep their power running.

Village Flute Playing

Flute playing in Pakistani villages is common. Animal grazers and herdsmen have flutes with them when taking their animals to graze. When the animals graze, the shepherd begins playing his flute to entertain himself and other shepherds who join him. This also announces to others that the shepherd is present. Those who keep their animals at their farms and guard them at night will remain awake and play the flute. This technique of playing the flute allows them to enjoy their nights on duty.

Village Nights

Village nights used to be very pleasant. Children played in the wide streets during the summer, and elders sat in the streets and chatted. Now there is fear and villagers return to their homes before sunset to remain inside for their security. In general, villagers eat dinner early because most villages do not have electricity, which has been turned off.

Sleeping

Village life is not as busy as city life, and so when a villager wants to sleep, he will go to bed early. Most villagers are called early birds because they enjoy getting up early. Afternoons are often spent sleeping under the shade of trees. The working class in the cities must follow strict work schedules, and so most do not sleep well until the weekend when they can enjoy sleeping. Oversleeping is considered laziness and it is discouraged.

Card Playing

Card playing is common both in villages and cities. People use their free time to play cards, and the elderly spend most of their time chatting and playing cards. That is their entertainment. During the summer, cards are played in the afternoon, and during the winter, whenever there is time, cards are played.

Pakistanis Think with the Heart

The simple people of Pakistan do not think with the brain, but instead, they feel and think with the heart. They do not have knowledge of modern sciences but they are caring and look for a leader who can think and feel with the heart and also feel the pain and suffering of the simple people. For them, he would a great leader.

Chaudry, Village Leader

A chaudry is a government-appointed village leader who is economically powerful and sometimes holds a district, provincial or national political office. As an appointed village head, he collects agricultural taxes for the government.

Village Watchman

Every village has a watchman who works under the supervision of the village administrator. Villagers pay the watchman something at the end of harvesting seasonal crops.

Village Messenger

Every village in Pakistan has a messenger who conveys important messages from the village administrator. He goes house to house with the messages. He also helps to maintain the house and farms of the village administrator and this is considered a low profile job.

Blacksmith

The blacksmith is a villager who is called to work by farmers. He is a worker (kumi) of the village and this is also a low profile job. The blacksmith helps to maintain the iron agricultural tools of farmers. His profession is hereditary, and his work is tough and demanding because most of it is done manually. He is paid well at the end of the crop season.

Carpenters

The carpenter, often under the auspices of a village administrator, works for farmers to make and repair wooden agricultural tools. He is paid in kind every year by the farmers, and he is not paid well. His job is considered a low profile job that is tough and demanding and is busy from morning to sunset.

Barefoot Walking

Similar to farmers working in the fields, a majority of village children and adults walk barefoot. They wear shoes during extreme winter conditions.

Transportation

In developed villages there is available transport of buses, taxis or wagons, but in a majority of villages, there is no proper public transportation.

Skinny Wrestler in the Village

In villages, for entertainment, people will call a very skinny person a wrestler. This title is given for fun. He is skinny and weak, but for fun he is called a wrestler.

Natural Lakes

Earlier, there were natural lakes near rivers that brought beauty to Pakistan. The lakes took the flowing water of the rivers during floods and this saved settlements from flood destruction. Now these natural lakes have been turned into developments, and when there are floods, the water flows into the developments and brings destruction.

Chenab, a River of Lovers

The river Chenab is one of five rivers in the province of Punjab, Pakistan, and this river is famous for stories of love. That is why it is called a river of lovers.

Milking Animals, Sign of Blessing

Families owning milk-producing animals are considered proud members of society because they have been blessed abundantly with milk and butter.

Animal Dealers

Animal dealing is a very profitable profession in Pakistan and there are animal dealers in every village and town. They buy young animals, raise them and sell them for a good price in the market, and they also buy older animals and sell them for a good profit.

Donkey

The donkey, a common animal in Pakistan, is a symbol of hard work. Those who work hard are called a donkey, which refers to working like a donkey.

The donkey is also a symbol of stupidity, and so, those who are not intelligent are called donkeys. In school, children who are not intelligent are also called donkeys by their teachers and even by their fellow students. Forty years ago, when parents took their children to school for admission, parents would tell the teachers they were giving them a donkey and they wanted their donkey to be made into a man. This was said mostly for male children.

The Buffalo, a Sign of Dullness

In Pakistan, because the buffalo is considered dull and not a wise and active animal, people considered dull will be called a buffalo. It is also a sign of laziness.

Jackal

The jackal is an animal that still exists near developments. It lives in crops or sugar cane fields or any hiding places. It eats peanuts and sugar cane and it also eats chickens. The people of Pakistan have a tolerant attitude toward the jackal because it is not a dangerous animal.

Wolf

The wolf used to be a common animal, but it is no longer common. It has either moved or been killed by the people. Wolves used to live near settlements and human beings could tolerate them, but with the passage of time, tolerance of wolves has decreased, especially because they are a threat to livestock and humans.

Flies

Flies are common in Pakistan and will be everywhere, in homes, sweet shops, small restaurants, and so forth. They are never killed and they are allowed to remain where they are. Items are generally covered as protection from the flies, but they are allowed to fly over and around them.

Snakes

The snake is common in Pakistan and it is a highly exploited. Everyone hates it except snake lovers who are called jogis. If a snake is seen, it is killed. There is no understanding, and so people kill them even though they may not be dangerous.

Quail Fighting Contests

Quail fighting is common in Pakistan. These fighting birds are well kept and well fed because the fighting is a source of income for the owner. A winner usually receives a cash prize.

Pigeon Flying Contests

Pigeon flying is a popular game in Pakistan. Pigeon lovers raise pigeons, feed them well, and train them to fly high and stay a long time in the air. In competitions, the winner is the pigeon that can fly the highest and stay the longest in the air. These pigeons have a variety of colors.

Pigeon Shrines

Pigeon shrines are a safe and good place for pigeons to live. These shines are not maintained by any organization, but people enjoy going to them to see the pigeons and to feed them. For this reason, the pigeons remain on the premises.

Camel Wrestling and Races

Camel wrestling is another form of entertainment in Pakistan. It is mostly organized during winter months, but it can be organized during any season. Camel lovers enjoy this wrestling even though camels can be dangerous. An angry camel can attack and even kill people. Usually, through, the wrestling is without incident.

Camels in the deserts of Pakistan are owned by settlers. When one is raised to race, it is given extra care and food and it is exercised more than the other camels. When a race is ready to happen, the camel is walked to the racing field to the rhythm of the drum as camel lovers dance to the beat.

Horse Races

Horses deemed qualified to run a race are owned by the rich who feed them well, even giving the horses milk and butter, and they are trained to run. They are taken to the racing stadium by means of a drum rhythm. The public can come to watch the race.

Bull Races

Bull races are common entertainment in Pakistani villages. Farmers raise and feed bulls well and then take them to annual, seasonal or regional races. Most races are organized by feudal farmers to provide entertainment for their tenants. By means of this entertainment, they keep their tenants united. The bulls are adorned with artificial decorations and bells and taken to the races with the rhythm of the drum, accompanied by the bull owner and his friends who dance.

Porcupine Quill, a Symbol of Fight

If a porcupine quill is left in someone's home, there will begin a continuous, nonstop fight. This is a gesture of transferring one's family fights to another house and family.

Mongoose and Snake Fights

Mongoose and snake fights are common and popular in Pakistan and people enjoy watching. They are raised by wild life experts who use them as a source of income.

Those who watch the fights generously give money to the owners and organizers of these fights.

Mongoose for House Protection

In Pakistan, the mongoose, a friendly animal, is a pet whose job is to protect the house night and day from snakes.

Cats and Dogs

Dogs work as house guards and cats protect the house from rats. Because there are no adoption agencies, if an owner has an extra dog, he can offer one.

Pets

People who have pets keep them mostly outdoors even during the rain, the cold of the winter, and the heat of the summer. They have to find shelter for themselves. Owners are only responsible for feeding them, and if they do not feed them, the pets have to find food by foraging in the neighborhood or hunting chickens.

Parrots

The parrot, called mian mathu, meaning a sweet creature, is a common pet in Pakistan. Those that can speak will entertain the family, friends and relatives. Most are green and reside in cages, but some are free to roam inside the house. Their wings are cut so they cannot leave.

Quail Hunting

Quail hunting is common and popular in rural areas of Pakistan. Quail lovers live mostly in villages and the quails they hunt are sold for good prices in the cities. The hunting is facilitated by using nets and traps. Quails are also raised at homes and sold as a business. They are very tasty when cooked with spices.

Fishing

There are professional and for fishermen who have a license to fish in rivers and seas.

Rabbit Hunting

Rabbit hunting is common in Pakistan throughout the year. One can see rabbit hunters on foot or on tractors hunting rabbits. After hunting, the rabbits are immediately killed with a prayer. They are delicious when cooked with spices.

CHAPTER 9

POVERTY AND WEALTH

Home Employees

Wealthy families employ dozens of workers paid less than twenty-five dollars per month. They work more than ten hours per day. The ratio of joblessness is so high that people are ready to work for low wages and under poor conditions.

Children as Housekeepers

In Pakistan, children are hired as housekeepers to work for low wages, and their salary goes to their parents. They are not enrolled in schools, but they are fed by their employers and occasionally they receive clothes and other needs.

Peons

Peons hold minor jobs in Pakistan. They are employed in schools and business offices as menial workers, and also they can be a personal employee of a head official to take care of personal needs.

Brick Factories

Brick factories are everywhere in Pakistan. The workers labor hard but are paid very little. Most have heavy loans held by the owners of the brick factories. Because the majority of workers are uneducated, it was easy to fool them into taking out a loan that they will never be able to pay back. They will be forever in debt.

Gardeners

Gardeners hold a minor position in Pakistan and they are poorly paid. They are employed by most schools and by government and non-government businesses to keep the landscape green.

Broom, Symbol of Disrespect

In Pakistan, a broom is a symbol of disrespect. Professional sweepers are considered and treated as outcasts because they use the broom. The profession of sanitation is considered discriminatory and disrespectful. At home, a woman using a broom for cleaning is acceptable, but if a male holds a broom, this is disrespectful. Outside the home it is disrespectful for both genders.

Trash Collectors

Trash collectors are professional, and they gather papers and plastic to sell to recycling companies. They are called 'changar' and they are not considered respectable. They are different from sanitary workers.

Relations and Business

Pakistan is a country of relationships as important as rules and regulations. A majority of business dealings are done on the basis of relations, and so, a good relationship must be apparent in order to form a deal. If a relationship cannot be proved, this indicates that one is dealing with a person who is not important.

Morning Shopkeeper Tradition

In the early morning, at the beginning of a business day, no credit is given to a customer because it is believed this could affect the entire day's business. To follow this tradition, a shopkeeper must turn his back to an early customer who needs credit in order to buy something.

Shopping Hours

In Pakistan, big and small shopping malls usually open after 11 a.m. or after 12 noon, and they will remain open until late at night. Street shops open early and close early. Small grocery stores close early.

Spending

Thirty years ago, it was common to see women shopping and spending in Pakistan, but now, because of an economic crisis, the attitude of women toward spending has changed dramatically. They cannot afford to spend because there is little money to spend. There is not enough income at home.

Bargaining

No matter what type of shopping is done, one can always bargain the prices or costs. Shopkeepers normally start with high prices, but if one walks away, then the shopkeepers are ready to bargain. There are no discount coupons, and so, if one wants a discount, one must bargain.

Attitude of Saving

In Pakistan, saving is not common because a majority of people are not paid well.

Therefore, they do not have much to save. What little they can save is put aside for emergencies, and often they must borrow money to deal with emergencies.

Stinginess

Stingy people are not very much liked in the society. Even stingy parents are not very much liked. Stinginess is understood as unkindness. They are not only unkind, but they do not worry about what is happening around them. They are not hated, but they are disliked.

Understanding Compromising

Pakistanis will compromise on any issue except issues involving honor and respect.

As mentioned earlier, land is a symbol of respect and so there is no compromise.

Also, any issue concerning the honor of a woman receives no compromise. A woman cannot be dishonored.

Punctuality

During my work with desert communities in Pakistan, I began everything punctually, and in time, the desert people I associated with appreciated this. Being late is common throughout Pakistan. The educated class feels honored to come late, and if a leader comes on time, he is not considered a leader. In short, nothing starts on time in Pakistan except military activities and Muslim prayers. I preferred to begin on time and the desert people quickly responded in a positive manner.

CHAPTER 10

CULTURAL BELIEFS

Greeting the Moon

Pakistanis like to greet the moon as a their maternal uncle, and so every Pakistani mother is a sister to the moon. People greet their moon uncle on the first day of his appearance.

Morning is Holy

Morning is holy in Pakistan, and so, talking about death or other unpleasant issues is inappropriate. Morning is to begin with positive thoughts. The elders will discourage any negative thought at the beginning of the day.

Evening is Holy

Evening is a holy time, and at the end of the day, no unpleasant issues are to be discussed. The day must end with happy and positive thoughts. Parents will discourage talk from anyone with negative thoughts.

Tuesday

In some cultures within Pakistan, Tuesday is not a good luck day, and so people do not sign or promise anything on Tuesday. They will not hold anything of importance on this day. For example, no marriage will take place on Tuesdays.

Wednesday

Wednesday is considered a lucky day. For example, if one receives a chance for a job interview on Wednesday, this is considered lucky because Wednesday keeps problems away. Wednesday is called a worry-free day

Thursday

Thursday is a day of saints. On this day, people who live apart from the normal world come to beg. The begging continues from morning to evening, and the public is ready to share food with these saintly people. They are not professional beggars but they have come from local shrines to collect food. It is part of their teachings to beg on Thursdays.

First Day of the Month

The first day of every month is very important. On this day no money or checks are issued. No bills are paid. Everything must be paid before or after the first day of every month. The meaning behind this thought is that the first day of the month should not start by giving because the whole month's process can be giving rather than receiving.

Thirteenth Month

January is called a thirteenth month in Pakistan by farmers. When desert farmers harvest their lentil crop at the end of the year, they invest their profits to grow new crops. And so, by the month of January, they are financially poor. They call January a thirteenth month because it involves finances, and Number 13 stands for a lack of financial resources.

First Day of the Year

The first day of the year is important in Pakistani culture. It should begin peacefully and end peacefully, and if it does not, then the year could be terrible because it could continue the way it was started. Disputes and disagreements are avoided on the first day of the year.

Difficult Days and Cultural Understanding

When unpleasant things happen during the same month, day, or week, this is considered unfortunate. There is a cultural way to deal with this. Food or other items can be donated to the poor or to religious leaders. It is believed this act will help protect the unfortunate from more unusual happenings.

Even Numbers, Lucky Numbers

Even numbers are considered lucky numbers. For example, if one is interviewed for a job on an even-numbered date, that would be considered lucky and fortunate.

Odd Numbers, Unlucky Numbers

Odd numbers are considered unlucky numbers in Pakistan. If any event falls on a date having an odd number, that will be considered unlucky.

Number 1

Number 1 stands for genuineness. It also stands for lonely, and so it is not good to be alone (one's self only). It is better to be in communion with someone.

Number 2

Number 2 stands for unity, power and communion, and it is said that two people are as powerful as eleven people—1 plus 1 equals 11. However, Number 2 does not represent quality. For example, a Number 2 place would be good enough to buy a newspaper or eat a quick sandwich.

Number 10

Number 10 stands for a person who has a bad reputation and is well known in the area. If he is caught by the police, they will number him 10 because of his poor and negative reputation.

Numbers 19 and 20

The numbers 19 and 20 are used to explain only a slight difference between two similar things or two living beings. For example, if there is only a little difference between two people, they have only a difference of 19 and 20.

Number 33

Thirty-three is the lowest passing mark for a student who sits for exams. It indicates he has barely passed.

Number 40

Pakistani culture believes that one is young until he reaches the age of forty. He is encouraged to eat in order to grow. However, at the age of forty, he is considered to be stepping into old age.

Number 90

This number symbolizes great loss. Working with an incapable person puts one in a position of losing, and so the chances of losing are 90%. It is beneficial only 10% of the time.

Number 420

This number stands for fraudulence. People who are frauds and who deceive, cheat and steal are called 420.

CHAPTER 11

OUTDOOR LIFE AND TRANSPORTATION

Vacationing

For a vacation, a majority of Pakistanis return home rather than going to hill stations or fun parks. Because of their deep attachment to their families, they prefer to be with them.

Shoes On Top Of Each Other Signal a Journey

Shoes on top of each other signal that a journey is expected. When families see shoes in this position, they know they might have to travel.

Picnics

Picnics are common in Pakistan, and most are enjoyed at rivers or canals. Some are held in parks. Picnics during the summer are fun for the rich and the poor who enjoy eating melons, watermelons and mangoes that are common during summer months. Picnickers, both rich and poor, can afford them.

Morning Walks

The morning walk is common in Pakistan but mostly the elderly will be seen taking walks in parks. Diabetic people like to walk.

Evening Walks

Evenings walks are common in Pakistan among the youth, children, parents and elderly. Youth walk after school hours. Young children walk with their parents.

Poor Transportation Facilities

A majority of Pakistanis travel by foot because they do not own motorcycles or cars. However, many have bicycles. There is public transportation in the cities, but in the villages there are poor transportation facilities, and so, people in the villages prefer to walk rather than waiting for transportation. In the cities, people also walk when they cannot afford to travel by public transport. The common man believes he does not have issues with diabetes, high blood pressure, high cholesterol and other health problems because of his daily walk.

Pedestrians

Pedestrians are not respected and have no rights. People who drive cars are powerful and can exploit the rights of pedestrians. Motorcyclists can do the same. When pedestrians wait to cross busy roads, no one pays attention.

Highways

Common Pakistanis traveling on highways do not like to read instructions and highway signs. They prefer to ask instructions from people because they believe this is a trustworthy source.

Accidents

Accidents are everywhere throughout Pakistan. The major causes are negligence and excessive speeding, people walking on most highways, and fog and rain.

Cyclist Rights

Bicycle riders have no rights, and cars, trucks, and bus drivers will show disrespect to them. Culturally, the cyclist is considered weak and so he must wait for the passing of motor drivers who are wealthy and therefore under no obligation to cyclists. Many cyclists die in motor accidents.

Horse Cart (Tonga) Owners

The horse cart is an affordable transport for the poor in both urban and rural areas. This is a demanding job for the drivers and they are not well paid. They have to work all day to feed their family and the horse. The horse is fed well every evening with chickpeas and fodder. Even though this transport is not safe, people continue to use it. It is difficult to manage a horse cart in modern traffic. There are hundreds who die because of horse cart accidents.

Bus Drivers

Bus driving is demanding. Drivers are hired by verbal contracts but they must have a driving license. Big transport companies have strict rules for drivers but local transport companies have more relaxed rules. Big transport companies pay drivers well, but local companies pay by the hour, which encourages excessive speeding.

Truck Drivers

Driving a truck in Pakistan is demanding. Drivers are paid well but they have to stay away from home for weeks or sometimes months. Because most trucks are not air-conditioned, in the summer truckers will wear loose pants and shirts while driving. People from the province of Pakhtoon Kha (formerly NWFP) know well the trucking business. Many own trucks or drive them.

Hawkers

Hawkers, or street peddlers, are generally at bus stations to entice potential customers to buy goods. Generally, they are well dressed; they work long hours; and they are not paid well. If one needs a bus ticket, he can buy one and secure a seat.

No Travel on Feast Days

Traveling on feast days is discouraged because it is considered unpleasant. That is why there is little transport available on feast days. Traveling is allowed if there is an emergency.

December and January, Cold Months

December and January are cold months and in the northern areas of Pakistan snow can be expected to begin in November and continue until March. The temperature sometimes drops below zero. People wear warm sweaters and jackets. 55 degrees Fahrenheit is normal in Central and South Pakistan.

During storms, wires and trees come down, roads are closed because of power outages, and there are traffic jams because of the lack of facilities to handle snow conditions. Driving in northern areas can be dangerous.

Interestingly, people in the northern areas do not eat spices to help keep warm. They prefer food that is similar to Western food. They drink much green tea in small cups to keep their bodies warm. When some hill stations in the south have snow, Pakistanis make snowmen.

Fog

December and January are foggy months. Sometimes the fog begins immediately after sunset and continues until noon the next day. This causes many accidents on the highways and even on back roads. Most schools close on foggy days. Robbers are very active during the foggy season.

Spring

Everybody loves spring when the weather is warm.

Summer

Mid April to mid September are extremely hot months and the temperature is often three digits. Many Pakistanis cover the necks and heads to avoid the risk of sunstroke.

Moon Nights

In Pakistan, moon nights are considered romantic. During the cold winter, moon nights may not be enjoyed, but summer moon nights are enjoyed with people staying awake, talking and enjoying themselves. Farmers are happy during moon nights because they do not have to water their fields in the dark. Children during summer moon nights like to play hide and seek. Accompanied girls and women go to the parks to enjoy the moon nights.

Rain

People of Pakistan do not like rain due to the poor drainage systems in the villages and cities.

Heel Rubbing and Prayers for Rain

Summers are tough if monsoons do not come and there is no rain. Most deserts remain dry during the summer, and so children sit in the heat of the sun to rub their heels and pray for rain. Sometimes the rains come and sometimes they do not, but heel rubbing is common practice in Pakistan.

Porridge Cooking for Rain

A common practice in desert villages is to cook porridge and distribute it to encourage rain during the summer. Villagers contribute towards cooking porridge, and this is also a form of prayer for rain.

Umbrellas

Using the umbrella in Pakistan is not common and only one pedestrian in a hundred will be seen carrying an umbrella during the rainy season or summer. Women cover their heads with their scarves and some men use caps, but not the majority. Farmers use turbans (parna) to protect their heads from the heat of the sun

Flamingos and Rain

When a group of flamingos fly east together, it is believed there will be rain. Villagers use this belief to predict rain during the summer.

Sparrows bring Rain

In the summer, if sparrows are seen taking a bath, this means it will rain. By taking a bath, they are asking for rain.

Pakistani sparrows are everywhere, and they spend their time in the fields enjoying eating wheat. They have nests inside and outside homes. People normally feed them by throwing leftover bread to them. They also enjoy eating raw wheat.

CHAPTER 12

ENTERTAINMENT

Music and the Pakistani Approach

It is commonly said that music nourishes the soul. Pakistanis love to hear and sing music, and yet, music is not considered to be a respectable profession. There is a contradiction here. Everyone enjoys music and at the same time there is rejection because music is not a respectable profession.

In cities, popular music is loudly played in teashops and restaurants to attract customers. In villages, sometimes loud speakers play music at weddings. Villagers like to carry a radio or tape recorder in order to enjoy music, and in cities, male youth will carry an iPod or Walkman to enjoy music.

Urban youth like pop and loud music; the elderly like semi-classical music; and village youth like folk music. When farmers water their fields at night, they loudly sing folk music, and when they plow their fields, they play loud music. Almost every activity is carried out with music in the background.

Folk Music

Folk music is equally liked by the educated and uneducated. It takes one deep into a reflection of one's self. It takes one far from the world and brings one back to the world. It is a powerful means to bring change in one's self and in the world. Folk music also brings a reflection of Nature.

Musical Compositions Not Written

Composers and musicians do not write music, and so, while arranging music, everything must be learned by heart. Music and compositions are preserved by recordings.

Classical Music Learning Not Easy

Because there are no classical music schools in Pakistan, those wishing to learn must join with someone who can teach them. There are no tuition fees and no books available, yet, a teacher of classical music can ask and demand things from his student, such as massages. If these demands can be met, the student will be given information on classical music. He must show sincerity to the teacher in order to obtain more and more learning.

Classical Music and Prayer

During education and learning of classical music, a student will wait and long for prayers and blessings from his teacher who may give them when he is satisfied with the student's learning and sincerity. This blessing may not make the student a superstar but he will be a successful classical artist.

Classical Music and Curse

Classical music and the music teacher must be respected by the student. Otherwise, the student can be cursed and he will be not be able to adopt classical music as his profession.

Musical Concerts in Villages

Villagers are very fond of music and they invite local singers to entertain them. While the singers are performing, villagers throw money on them as a means of showing appreciation. These performances continue all night accompanied by tea or seasonal drinks. A majority of villagers like fast folk songs for dancing and enjoying themselves.

Folk Singing

Folk music is the most popular form of music in Pakistan, and it is especially popular among villagers. Pakistanis entertain themselves by listening to folk singers and music. Sometimes folk singers are invited to villages to attend marriages or social parties. Sometimes the villagers go to local shrines to receive social, religious and cultural nourishment.

Desert Music

Desert people like to sing. Music is the only entertainment. Because desert people suffer from a daily lack of basic facilities, this pain can be felt in their music.

In the deserts of Punjab there is Cholistani, Saraiki and Marwari influence in their music which combines three different spiritual and cultural traditions. It connects desert tribes.

Parat Playing

At weddings and family celebrations, a parat, a rice container made of silver, is played in a rhythmic manner by a woman who holds it on her lap and leads women singing wedding songs.

The Pitcher

Pitcher playing at weddings, engagements and other celebrations is common in villages. Women provide this entertainment very well. One has a slipper in her hand to beat rhythmically the mouth of a pitcher and another woman beats the pitcher with a stone. The sound produced is stimulating.

Dancing

Culturally, dancing is a popular in Pakistan, and a majority of Pakistanis love to dance. Not only do children, adults and the elderly love to dance, but they also love to watch dancing. There are highly professional dancers in Pakistan. However, culturally the dance is not recognized as a respectable profession or art. Adopting this profession is not encouraged. Nevertheless, professional dancers will remain brave and keep this art alive regardless of all cultural and religious challenges they face.

Comedians

Most Pakistani weddings have invited comedians or they come without invitation. They provide entertainment and they joke spontaneously with guests, including the bridegroom. Comedians do not joke with women, but they will target every male. In appreciation for a good performance, guests give them money, and they can usually expect to be given free food.

Rice

In order to create a friendly environment, people are entertained with rice before they are given an informal education on political, religious, and social matters.

People love to participate in activities where rice is served. Education after a meal is ineffective because people tend to leave after eating.

Fairs

Fairs are celebrated with food, music and dancing throughout Pakistan, but most are organized at shrines. People wearing clean and good clothes go to these fairs not only for entertainment but also for prayers and personal and family intentions.

CHAPTER 13

DECEASED FAMILY RELATIVES

Honor and Respect

A Pakistani is ready to die for the honor and respect of his family. This stands above everything, and by adulthood it has been fixed into the mind of the male that he is guardian of the family's honor and respect. He is trained to be brave, and he will die protecting his family. He understands that women and property are valuable, and they need to be protected so the family can enjoy dignity.

Donating Parts of Body

Donating parts of a body in Pakistan is not common. The concept of perfection is very strong even after death. People want their body to be perfect, and so it is difficult for a family to see their loved one without some parts of the body. For this reason, the majority of people and families do not like to donate body parts.

Women and Funerals

Funerals are arranged by male family members. Women are not given this responsibility and they must stay within the four walls of the house and mourn. When the funeral procession is ready, male family members and others will accompanied it to the graveyard because culturally, it is not respectful for women to walk in the streets.

Coffin

The coffin is generally provided by the family, and it is customary for the parents to make arrangements for the coffin. The color is mostly white, but some families will choose different colors. A green and black sheet is often used to cover the coffin. The Christians in Pakistan use white sheets.

Graves are Free of Cost

It is the responsibility of the government of Pakistan to provide graveyards, and so people do not have to worry about making arrangements for the grave for their loved one. The family only has to pay for the coffin and the gravediggers.

Silent Cities

Graveyards are lonely and barren, usually far from developments, and not well kept. There is little greenery in them. Most of the graves are made of mud, but some are made of concrete if people can afford it. Graveyards are visited by people during festivals, and also the graves of loved ones are visited during the year. It is believed that the spirits of the dead walk in the graveyards, and so it is not advisable to visit them at night. Because of fear, it is also believed that graveyards should not be visited alone.

Graveyard Caretakers

If you happen to visit Pakistani graveyards or memorial parks, you will find people living there. Most live permanently in the graveyards. They have abandoned the world and have decided to live a life apart from the world. They wear long beards and long shirts, and they do not work, but instead, they depend on food provided by people whose loved ones are buried there. Sometimes people living in the graveyards have food with them and even do some cooking, but most of the time they beg. Food is given to these grave caretakers by families expecting a prayer from them for their loved ones, and also they give food for the cleaning of the graves.

Understanding of Consolation

The value of consolation is strong in Pakistan, and people step forward to console when there is need. Consolation is done by physical presence and verbally. There are certain gestures, such as sitting or standing calmly shows consolation. Listening patiently also communicates care and consolation. Another gesture is the bringing of food to console a loved one.

CHAPTER 14

FOLKLORE

Picture Falling

If a picture of a loved one is hanging on the wall and it falls, that is a sign that something unfortunate will happen.

Glass/Mirror Breaking

If any dish made of glass is broken, that is a sign of misfortune, and so people are careful when holding dishes made of glass.

Bed Breaking

If one is sitting on a bed and it breaks, this is considered unfortunate for the person sitting on the bed. That is why people keep beds in good shape. A bed that breaks is also a sign of disrespect.

Sweet Eatables

Generally, people do not accept and eat sweet things from strangers or people they suspect. It is believed that these sweet eatables can be used for revenge and they have been blessed by a magician. If eaten, a business or person can be destroyed.

Uncooked Meat in a Dream

Seeing uncooked meat in a dream is unfortunate because it signifies that something unpleasant will happen. To avoid such a dream, food or sweets are distributed among the people. People also like to offer lamb to a religious leader with the hope of protection from any unpleasant event.

Uncooked Meat and Demons

It is believed that if one carries uncooked meat and walks through a forest, demons will begin following because they like to eat meat. They will cause trouble.

Trees and Demons

It is also commonly believed in Pakistan that there are demons active in trees in the evening, and so, by shaking or going under trees, this could cause serious trouble. Therefore, elders advise not to shake or go under trees in the evening.

Snakes and Dreams

If live snakes are seen in dreams, it is not a good sign because this may signal a bringing of bad news or a test for the family. If a dead snake is seen, it means that evil is dead and so there is no longer a danger to the family.

Crying of a Dog

A crying dog is not a good sign. If it cries in the evening or at night, this will not good bring good news to the family. If someone dies in or outside the family, it would be understood why the dog is crying. The family does not check to see if the crying dog is hungry or sick.

Black Cats

A black cat is not lucky. It is believed that if a person is intent on doing something important and a black cat walks in front of him, this is considered unfortunate.

The Dead in Dreams

If dead ones are seen in dreams, this means that the dead ones have come to take the dreamer with them. This is a message of death, and many people become afraid and interpret these dreams as a warning.

Do Not Call To Someone Leaving The House

In Pakistan, people do not call to someone who has left the house, because calling to him can bring misfortune. If, by mistake, the person is called, then he must return and sit for a time before leaving again.

Remembering Dreams

Women believe that if one can remember a dream, there is a meaning to the dream that needs to be found.

Fruit and Dreams

If a Pakistani sees fruit in dreams, it means prosperity and hope. Any type of fruit in dreams brings good news to the person or to the family. If plenty of fruit is seen in dreams, it means that the family will be blessed with prosperity.